Usborne

Roman patterns to colour

Illustrated by David Thelwell
Designed by Emily Beevers
Written by Sam Baer

Ancient Romans

Over 2,000 years ago, the Ancient Romans ruled over much of Europe and beyond. They were famous for their powerful army, but they had skilled engineers and craftspeople too, creating many things, from delicate jewellery to grand temples.

This mosaic shows a guilloche (braided) pattern.

Borders were often made from patterns of cresting waves...

...or repeated triangles.

Roman patterns

The Romans used *mosaics* – pictures and patterns made from small pieces of stone – to decorate floors. They also painted bright pictures on their walls with paints and dyes made from plants, insects and minerals.

Dressing up

Wealthy Romans wore brightly dyed clothes, accessorized with ornate jewellery. Gold jewellery was moulded into shape, then studded with precious stones or carved with intricate patterns.

This necklace has snake heads on either end.

Signs and symbols

Patterns often featured important signs and symbols, many of which came from Roman stories, and had very specific meanings.

The head of a snake-haired woman was thought to protect against evil.

The eagle was thought to be a symbol of power.

Public art

Many public buildings were supported by grand pillars, known as *columns*, with intricately carved tops, called *capitals*. Capitals were often highly decorated with flowers and leaves.

This column is topped with patterns made from leaves and winged horses.

Painted homes

In the homes of wealthy Romans, each room was decorated with wall paintings, known as *frescoes*. They were often brightly coloured, with red, yellow and blue paints being especially popular.

This wall painting is based on a fresco found in Pompeii, Italy. It was preserved when the city was buried in ash by a huge volcanic eruption almost 2,000 years ago.
This bird's tail is blue and green.
Colour this snake red and green.
Snakes were often kept as pets, to eat mice.

Lavish containers

Roman craftspeople made grand containers out of glass, clay and metal. Containers varied in size and shape, from tiny perfume bottles to huge vases.

This *ribbon glass* jug was made by heating strips of different coloured glass in a mould until they melted and fused together.
Colour the patterns on this bronze vase blue, green and red.
Small glass bottles stored perfumes, oils or medicines. The patterns on this bottle are designed to look like budding leaves.
These handles were designed to look like dolphins.
The different strips of glass are blue, green, yellow and red.

Mosaic tiles

These pictures, called mosaics, are made up of tiny coloured stones. Each one features a different type of animal – dolphins, a panther, a lion, a peacock and a rabbit.

Grand buildings

The Romans built magnificent buildings, monuments and tombs, covered with striking patterns and motifs.

The roofs of many buildings were supported by stone columns. The top of a column, known as its capital, was often elaborately carved.

These capitals combine flowers, acanthus leaves and swirls.

This carved panel is from a type of wall decoration known as a *pilaster*.

Dressed to impress

Most Roman clothing has decayed and disappeared over time, but carvings, statues and frescoes show us what it looked like.

Emperors and successful generals wore golden crowns made to look like laurel wreaths.
Ornate armour was a symbol of power.
Colour this cape red with a gold trim.
Women often wore a shawl or *palla* over a simple dress known as a *stola*.
Men wore robes known as *togas*. Most were undyed, but the hems of politicians' togas were coloured with expensive purple dye.

Coloured gems

Roman men and women completed their outfits with dazzling jewellery, studded with coloured glass or precious gems.

The gems on this gold bracelet are emeralds and sapphires. Colour them green and blue.

Gold rings and bracelets in the form of snakes were very popular.

The bands of this multicoloured bracelet are shaped to look like ivy leaves.

The beads on these earrings are made from blue and red glass.

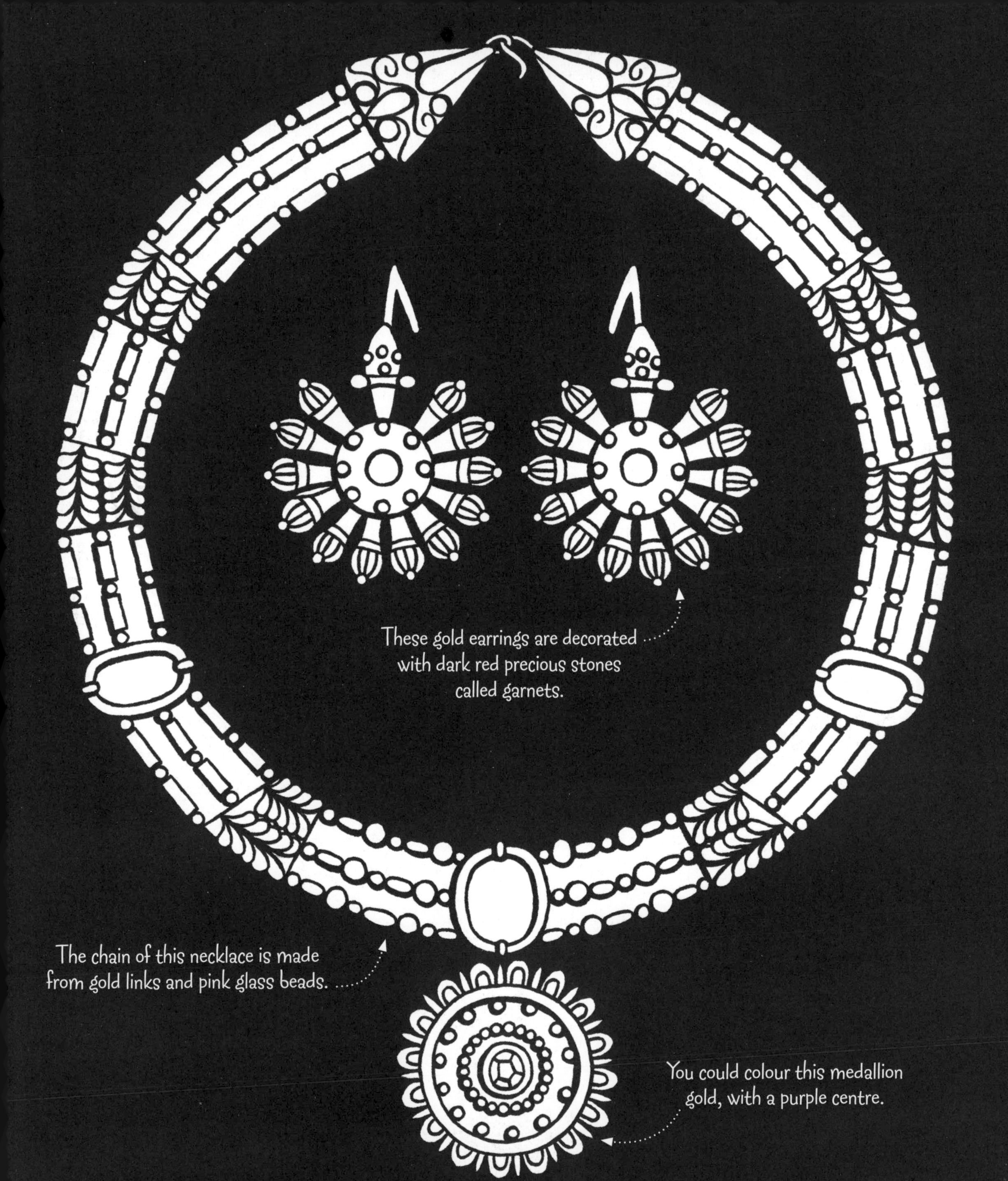
These gold earrings are decorated
with dark red precious stones
called garnets.
The chain of this necklace is made
from gold links and pink glass beads.
You could colour this medallion
gold, with a purple centre.

After life

When rich Romans died, their remains were sometimes placed in stone coffins decorated with intricate patterns, like the ones on these pages.

Gods and goddesses

The Romans worshipped hundreds of gods and goddesses. These scenes, taken from carved stone coffins, show some of the most important.

This scene shows the story of Luna, goddess of the moon, who fell in love with a sleeping man named Endymion.

Juno, on the left, was queen of the gods and protector of Rome. Jupiter, in the centre, was king of the gods and god of thunder. Minerva, to the right, was the goddess of wisdom.

Mythical creatures

The Romans believed the world was home to all kinds of strange and fantastic creatures. This is *Pegasus* – a graceful winged horse.

Roman musician
The stringed instr
with a pick. B

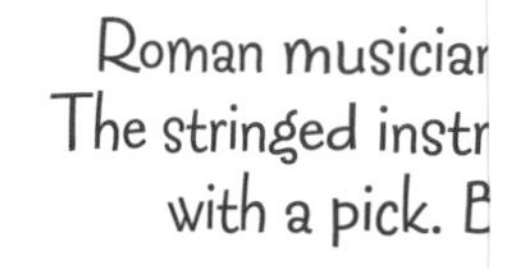

Pipes

Hippocamps were horse-like sea creatures. Colour this one green and red.

This three-headed dog, known as *Cerberus*, has bright red eyes.

Half-eagle, half-lion creatures known as *griffins* were loyal guardians. These griffins are red and yellow with blue wings.

Romans loved to se
Performers
Grim-looking masks were worn for tragedies.

Edited by Emily Bone. First published in 2015 by Usborne Publishing, Usborne House, 83-85 Saffron Hill, London EC1N 8RT, England. www.usborne.com

For links to websites where you can see patterns on Roman artefacts, go to the Usborne Quicklinks website at www.usborne.com/quicklinks and enter the keywords 'Roman patterns'. Please follow the internet safety guidelines at the Usborne Quicklinks website.